peace

Other Studies in the Fruit of the Spirit Bible Study Series

Faithfulness: The Foundation of True Friendship
Gentleness: The Strength of Being Tender
Joy: How to Rejoice in Any Situation
Kindness: Reaching Out to Others
Love: Building Healthy Relationships
Patience: The Benefits of Waiting
Self-Control: Mastering Our Passions

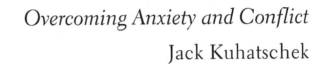

peace

Overcoming Anxiety and Conflict

Jack Kuhatschek

ZONDERVAN®

ZONDERVAN.com/
AUTHORTRACKER
follow your favorite authors

ZONDERVAN

Peace: Overcoming Anxiety and Conflict
Copyright © 1991, 2001 by Jack Kuhatschek

Requests for information should be addressed to:

Zondervan, *Grand Rapids, Michigan* 49530

ISBN 978-0-310-23869-0

Interior design by Melissa Elenbaas

Printed in the United States of America

09 10 11 12 13 14 15 16 • 30 29 28 27 26 25 24 23 22 21 20 19 18 17 16 15 14 13 12

CONTENTS

Fruit of the Spirit Bible Studies   7

Peace: Overcoming Anxiety and Conflict   9

one   Coping with Anxiety   11
       Philippians 4:4–9

two   Why We Shouldn't Worry   17
       Matthew 6:25–34

three Finding Peace in God's Presence   23
       Psalm 46

four   Feeling Safe in God's Care   29
       Psalm 91

five   Living at Peace with Others   35
       Romans 12:17–21

six   Christ, Our Peace   41
       Ephesians 2:11–22

       Leader's Notes   47

FRUIT OF THE SPIRIT
BIBLE STUDIES

Welcome to Fruit of the Spirit Bible Studies. This series was written with one goal in mind—to allow the Spirit of God to use the Word of God to produce his fruit in your life.

To get the most from this series you need to understand a few basic facts:

Fruit of the Spirit Bible Studies are designed to be flexible. You can use them in your quiet times or for group discussion. They are ideal for Sunday school classes, small groups, or neighborhood Bible studies.

The eight guides in this series can be used in any order that is best for you or your group.

Because each guide contains only six studies, you can easily explore more than one fruit of the Spirit. In a Sunday school class, any two guides can be combined for a quarter (twelve weeks), or the entire series can be covered in a year.

Each study deliberately focuses on only one or two passages. That allows you to see each passage in its context, avoiding the temptation of prooftexting and the frustration of "Bible hopscotch" (jumping from verse to verse). If you would like to look up additional passages, a Bible concordance will give the most help.

The questions help you *discover* what the Bible says rather than simply *telling* you what it says. They encourage you to think and to explore options rather than to merely fill in the blanks with one-word answers.

Leader's notes are provided in the back of the guide. They show how to lead a group discussion, provide additional information on questions, and suggest ways to deal with problems that may come up in the discussion. With such helps, someone with little or no experience can lead an effective study.

SUGGESTIONS FOR INDIVIDUAL STUDY

1. Begin each study with prayer. Ask God to help you understand the passage and to apply it to your life.
2. A good modern translation, such as the *New International Version,* the *New American Standard Bible,* or the *Revised Standard Version,* will give you the most help. However, the questions in this guide are based on the *New International Version.*
3. Read and reread the passage(s). You must know what the passage says before you can understand what it means and how it applies to you.
4. Write your answers in the space provided in the study guide. This will help you to clearly express your understanding of the passage.
5. Keep a Bible dictionary handy. Use it to look up any unfamiliar words, names, or places.

SUGGESTIONS FOR GROUP STUDY

1. Come to the study prepared. Careful preparation will greatly enrich your time in group discussion.
2. Be willing to join in the discussion. The leader of the group will not be lecturing but will encourage people to discuss what they have learned in the passage. Plan to share what God has taught you in your individual study.
3. Stick to the passage being studied. Base your answers on the verses being discussed rather than on outside authorities such as commentaries or your favorite author or speaker.
4. Try to be sensitive to the other members of the group. Listen attentively when they speak, and be affirming whenever you can. This will encourage more hesitant members of the group to participate.
5. Be careful not to dominate the discussion. By all means, participate! But allow others to have equal time.
6. If you are the discussion leader, you will find additional suggestions and helpful ideas in the leader's notes at the back of the guide.

PEACE

Overcoming Anxiety and Conflict

I am afraid of heights. I have been known to crawl on my hands and knees to the edge of a high balcony in order to look down. Imagine, then, how I felt when a camp director told me I had to rappel down the side of a steep cliff. "Everyone does it," he said matter-of-factly. "It's part of our program."

With sweaty palms and pounding heart, I eased backwards off the edge of the cliff, supported by a rope and a safety line. In order to walk down the face of the cliff, I was told to keep my body perpendicular to the cliff. Every nerve and fiber screamed at me to straighten up, to get in a vertical, not a horizontal position. Yet those who did so lost their footing and were left dangling high above the ground. Only by fighting my natural urges, and by trusting the ropes and those who held them, did I manage to make it safely to the bottom. What a relief!

That fearful experience of rappeling has become a parable of faith to me. There have been many times in my life when God has asked me to ease over the edge of a cliff, to trust him for something that seemed unsafe and frightening. The primary difference, of course, is that both the safety rope and the person at the top of the cliff are invisible—while the cliff and its dangers are in plain sight!

In order to fight my natural urges and to obey what God was calling me to do, I have had to go to Scripture again and again. I have read and reread those passages that assure me of God's presence and support. God is the one who holds the rope, they tell me, and he will never let me fall.

This study guide explores six of those passages—the ones that have been most helpful to me during times of anxiety and conflict. The peace they offer is not a permanent possession. Rather, it is experienced afresh with each new challenge. My prayer is that by reading and meditating on them, you will grow in your trust of "the God who holds in his hand your life and all your ways" (Dan. 5:23).

COPING WITH ANXIETY

Philippians 4:4–9

Garrison Keillor, author of *Lake Wobegon Days,* writes that his greatest fear as a child was of getting his tongue stuck on a frozen pump handle. The older boys told him that if he touched his tongue to a pump handle, the only way to get him loose would be to rip his tongue right out of his mouth or else put a tent over him until spring.

We all suffer from fears and anxieties of various sorts. Yet if we fail to deal with our anxieties, they can cripple and immobilize us. In Philippians 4, Paul gives us a prescription for inner peace.

Warming Up

1. What sorts of things make you feel anxious?

Digging In

2.   Read Philippians 4:4–9. Paul begins by telling us repeatedly to "rejoice in the Lord always" (v. 4). What does it mean to rejoice in the Lord?

Why is this kind of rejoicing possible in any circumstances?

3.   Why is prayer (v. 6) our first and best defense against anxiety?

4.   Why is it important to be thankful in the midst of our requests?

5.   Paul compares the peace of God to a sentry guarding our hearts
      and minds from anxiety (v. 7). Why do you think Paul adds that
      God's peace "transcends all understanding"?

6.   Anxious people can become obsessed with negative thinking. How
      can focusing on the good things in verse 8 free us from the grip of
      anxiety?

7. Give specific examples of the kinds of good things you might think about to combat anxiety.

8. According to verse 9, what is our third defense against anxiety?

9. How can observing the godly example of others and putting into practice what we see bring greater peace to our lives?

10.   What anxious thoughts have troubled you recently?

Pray about It

Take time now to bring your anxieties to God in prayer. Remember to thank him for what he has already done and for what he will do for you in the future.

TAKING THE NEXT STEP

During anxious times, the psalmist encourages us to remember what God has done for us in the past (see Pss. 77; 105; 143). Read one or more of these psalms. Then take time to remember some of the ways God has helped, strengthened, or delivered you in the past. Allow his faithfulness to fill your mind and heart in the present.

WHY WE SHOULDN'T WORRY

Matthew 6:25–34

Don't worry. Be happy." These words of a popular song are fun to sing, but they provide no real help to the worrier. Telling an anxious person not to worry is like telling a cold, hungry person to be warmed and filled. Why shouldn't we worry when we face the daily pressure of providing food and clothing for ourselves and our families?

In Matthew 6:25–34 Jesus does more than simply telling us not to worry. He tells us *why* we shouldn't worry.

Warming Up

1. What are some common reasons why people worry?

Digging In

2.   Read Matthew 6:25–34. What, specifically, does Jesus tell us not
      to worry about (vv. 25, 28, 31–32)?

      Which of these, if any, causes the greatest anxiety in your life?
      Why?

3.   In what sense is life more important than food, and the body more
      important than clothes (v. 25)?

4.   According to Jesus, how can we be confident that the Father will feed us and clothe us (vv. 26–30)?

5.   Many people, including some Christians, have little food to eat and are dressed much worse than Solomon, not to mention the lilies. How, then, are we to understand Christ's assurances about food and clothes?

6.   In what ways have you seen God provide for your basic needs?

7.   According to verse 27, why is it futile to worry?

If worry is a waste of time and energy, then why do you think it is such a popular pastime?

8.   In what sense are we acting like pagans when we fret about food or clothing (vv. 31–32)?

When you are anxious, how does it help you to know that your heavenly Father knows your needs (v. 32)?

9.   In contrast to pagan pursuits, what does it mean to "seek first his kingdom and his righteousness" (v. 33)?

10. According to Jesus, why is it best to take one day at a time (v. 34)?

Pray about It

Thank the Father for the way he cares and provides for our basic needs. Ask him to help you to act less like a pagan worrier and more like a kingdom seeker.

TAKING THE NEXT STEP

When we worry about the future, we are fighting with "ghosts"—things that do not exist and which may never exist. Instead of expending energy and anxiety on these phantoms, ask God to give you grace for what you are facing today and today only. Leave the unknown future in his hands.

three

FINDING PEACE IN GOD'S PRESENCE

Psalm 46

The eye of a hurricane is a remarkable place. Fierce, destructive winds spiral around it at terrifying speeds. Torrential rains encircle it, bringing floods and pounding waves. But within the eye itself, everything is calm and peaceful—a quiet refuge in the midst of the storm.

Psalm 46 describes such a place, a spiritual haven from the destructive forces that sometimes surround us.

Warming Up

1. What frightens you most about such natural forces as hurricanes, tornados, and earthquakes?

Digging In

2.   Read Psalm 46. What portrait of God emerges from verse 1?

3.   As you read verses 2–3, what images come to mind?

4.   What kinds of personal events can make us feel like the world is falling apart around us?

5.   How does the scene described in verses 4–5 contrast with the pre-
        vious scene?

        What aspects of the city of God seem most inviting to you?

6.   Verses 7 and 11 describe God as our fortress. What purposes does
        a fortress serve in wartime?

How is it reassuring to know that our fortress is the Lord Almighty?

7. Verses 6–10 also describe the Lord as a warrior. What effect does he have on the battles among nations?

8. What active role does he take in the battles we face in life (see, for example, Rom. 8:26–27; 1 Cor. 10:13; 2 Cor. 1:3–11; Eph. 6:10–18)?

9.   In our active, take-charge culture, the command to "be still" (v. 10) seems completely out of place. What does it mean to *be still* before God?

How can our obedience to this command bring about a more exalted view of God?

Pray about It

Think of the battles you are currently facing. How can you allow the Lord to be both your fortress and your warrior in those battles? Bring those battles to him in prayer.

TAKING THE NEXT STEP

Find a quiet place where you can be alone with God. It can be a favorite room in your house, a coffee shop, a park, or a garden. Bring your Bible with you and spend time reading and meditating on Psalm 46. Imagine yourself sitting by one of the streams that bring joy to the city of God, the holy place where the Most High dwells. Praise God for his peace and protection.

FEELING SAFE IN GOD'S CARE

Psalm 91

In 1956 Jim Elliot and four other missionaries were killed by the Auca Indians. Later, his widow, Elizabeth, wrote about the events leading up to Jim's death in a book entitled *Shadow of the Almighty*. The title was taken from Psalm 91 which, ironically, promises God's protection for those who trust in him. The sweeping promises of the psalm force us to wrestle with a nagging question: How can we feel safe in God's care in a world where bad things happen to good people?

Warming Up

1.   When you were a child, what made you feel safe and secure?

Digging In

2.   Read Psalm 91. What images does the psalmist use to describe
      God's protective care?

3.   How does each image affect your feeling of safety?

4.   What types of danger are mentioned in the psalm?

What modern-day counterparts might we face?

5.   Is the psalmist really promising that nothing bad will happen to those who trust in God? Explain.

6.   In Luke 4:10–11 Satan applies the promise of this psalm to Jesus. Yet how do Christ's own experiences cause us to examine the type of protection God offers?

7.   What does it mean to make the Most High our "dwelling" and
      "refuge" (v. 9)?

8.   Verses 9–13 speak of God's commanding his angels to guard us.
      How do you respond to the idea that you have guardian angels?

Have you ever sensed their presence in the midst of danger?
Explain.

9. In verses 14–16 the psalmist becomes silent and God speaks. Read these verses to yourself, substituting your name for the pronouns *he* and *him*.

How does it make you feel to have the Lord speak to you in that way?

10. What current circumstances make you feel unsafe or vulnerable?

How does this psalm help you to feel safer in God's care?

Pray about It

Bring your current circumstances to the Lord in prayer. Thank him for being your dwelling and refuge.

TAKING THE NEXT STEP

The psalmist describes the Lord as a refuge, fortress, mother bird, shield, rampart, and dwelling. Which of these images make you feel protected and safe? Meditate on those images, imagining yourself under God's protection. Since these images are not fiction but reality, how should your life be different this week and beyond:

at work?
financially?
as you face the future?
in your family?
other?

LIVING AT PEACE WITH OTHERS

Romans 12:17–21

One day a man dumped a large load of garbage into the creek behind the house of a friend of mine. As my friend was cleaning up the soggy mess, he noticed an envelope with the man's name and address on it. He promptly loaded up the garbage and drove to the man's house. Just as the man was coming out his front door, my friend dumped the entire pile of garbage into his front yard. The man stood there dumbfounded as my friend drove away laughing.

Was my friend right or wrong in his action? Romans 12:17–21 gives us guidelines for responding to those who mistreat us.

Warming Up

1. How would you have responded if someone had dumped a load of garbage in your yard? Why?

Digging In

2.   Read Romans 12:17–21. Why are we often tempted to repay evil
       for evil?

3.   Give examples of some of the ways people and countries repay evil
       for evil.

How does revenge frequently make things worse rather than better?

4. Paul commands us to live at peace with everyone—with two qual-
    ifications: "if it is possible" and "as far as it depends on you" (v. 18).
    Why are these qualifications important?

5. Why do you think God forbids us to take revenge, reserving
    vengeance for himself (v. 19; see also Deut. 32:35)?

6. How can the promise of God's wrath help restrain our desire for
    revenge?

7.   In verse 20 Paul quotes Proverbs 25:21–22. What is radical about the advice of this proverb?

8.   What do you think it means to "heap burning coals" on our enemy's head (v. 20; see also Prov. 25:21–22)?

9.   In addition to giving food and water to our enemy, what are some other ways we might overcome evil with good (v. 21)?

10. Think of someone who has recently mistreated you. What might you do to promote peace with that person?

Pray about It

Spend time now praying for the person who has mistreated you, asking God to help you overcome evil with good.

TAKING THE NEXT STEP

Make a genuine effort this week to do something kind and gracious to the person who has mistreated you. Let it be a first step in living at peace with him or her.

CHRIST, OUR PEACE

Ephesians 2:11–22

In *The Adventures of Huckleberry Finn*, Huck visits Tom's Aunt Sally. She immediately begins probing him about why he arrived so late:

"We been expecting you a couple of days and more. What kep' you?—boat get aground?"

"Yes'm ... but it warn't the grounding—that didn't keep us back but a little. We blowed out a cylinder head."

"Good gracious! Anybody hurt?"

"No'm. Killed a nigger."

Racial prejudice has always plagued humanity. But our hostility runs deeper than race. National pride, ethnic superiority, class distinctions, religious bigotry—each one drives a wedge between us and our neighbor. In Ephesians 2, Paul explains how Christ has demolished the barriers that divide us.

Warming Up

1. Why do you think people often feel a need to distinguish between "us" and "them"?

Digging In

2.   Read Ephesians 2:11–22. The Jews called the Gentiles "uncir-
      cumcised" (v. 11) and even referred to them as "dogs" (Matt.
      15:26). What labels do people today apply to those who are dif-
      ferent from them?

      What is wrong with such labels?

3.   In what ways were the Gentiles truly separated from the Jews
      (v. 12)?

4. In what ways are non-Christians today truly separated from Christians?

5. What did Christ do to end the hostility and separation between Jews and Gentiles (vv. 13–18)?

6. Why does Christ's death destroy all the racial, ethnic, and social distinctions that often separate us from others?

7.   What do we now have in common with everyone who is "in Christ"—even with those whom we formerly despised (vv. 14–22)?

8.   In what sense, if any, does Christ bring peace between us and those who do not yet know him?

9.   If we are truly one in Christ with all who know him, then why are so many churches divided on the basis of race, ethnic origin, and social status?

10.   What might we do to encourage greater diversity in our churches?

11.   What might you do in your family to encourage greater accep-
      tance of those who are different?

Pray about It

Think of one way in which prejudice is still a problem for you. Ask God
to allow the fruit of peace to overcome that prejudice.

TAKING THE NEXT STEP

What ethnic groups or minorities in your area are looked down on or despised? Take a piece of paper and divide it into two columns. In the left column make a list of some of the reasons for this prejudice. In the right column record what Christ has done to overcome each item in your list. How should that reality affect your relationship with these people?

LEADER'S NOTES

Leading a Bible discussion—especially for the first time—can make you feel both nervous and excited. If you are nervous, realize that you are in good company. Many biblical leaders, such as Moses, Joshua, and the apostle Paul, felt nervous and inadequate to lead others (see, for example, 1 Cor. 2:3). Yet God's grace was sufficient for them, just as it will be for you.

Some excitement is also natural. Your leadership is a gift to the others in the group. Keep in mind, however, that other group members also share responsibility for the group. Your role is simply to stimulate discussion by asking questions and encouraging people to respond. The suggestions listed below can help you to be an effective leader.

PREPARING TO LEAD

1. Ask God to help you understand and apply the passage to your own life. Unless that happens, you will not be prepared to lead others.
2. Carefully work through each question in the study guide. Meditate and reflect on the passage as you formulate your answers.
3. Familiarize yourself with the leader's notes for the study. These will help you understand the purpose of the study and will provide valuable information about the questions in the study.
4. Pray for the various members of the group. Ask God to use these studies to bring about greater spiritual fruit in the life of each person.

5. Before the first meeting, make sure each person has a study guide. Encourage them to prepare beforehand for each study.

LEADING THE STUDY

1. Begin the study on time. If people realize that the study begins on schedule, they will work harder to arrive on time.

2. At the beginning of your first time together, explain that these studies are designed to be discussions not lectures. Encourage everyone to participate, but realize that some may be hesitant to speak during the first few sessions.

3. Read the introductory paragraph at the beginning of the discussion. This will orient the group to the passage being studied.

4. Read the passage aloud. You may choose to do this yourself, or you might ask for volunteers.

5. The questions in the guide are designed to be used just as they are written. If you wish, you may simply read each one aloud to the group. Or you may prefer to express them in your own words. However, unnecessary rewording of the questions is not recommended.

6. Don't be afraid of silence. People in the group may need time to think before responding.

7. Avoid answering your own questions. If necessary, rephrase a question until it is clearly understood. Even an eager group will quickly become passive and silent if they think the leader will do most of the talking.

8. Encourage more than one answer to each question. Ask, "What do the rest of you think?" or "Anyone else?" until several people have had a chance to respond.

9. Try to be affirming whenever possible. Let people know you appreciate their insights into the passage.

10. Never reject an answer. If it is clearly wrong, ask, "Which verse led you to that conclusion?" Or let the group handle the problem by asking them what they think about the question.

11. Avoid going off on tangents. If people wander off course, gently bring them back to the passage being considered.

12. Conclude your time together with conversational prayer. Ask God to help you apply those things that you learned in the study.

13. End on time. This will be easier if you control the pace of the discussion by not spending too much time on some questions or too little on others.

Many more suggestions and helps are found in the book *Leading Bible Discussions* (InterVarsity Press). Reading that would be well worth your time.

Study 1

COPING WITH ANXIETY

Philippians 4:4–9

Purpose: To understand what is required to know the peace of God and the God of peace.

Question 1. Every study begins with an "approach question," which is discussed *before* reading the passage. An approach question is designed to do three things.

First, it helps to break the ice. Because an approach question doesn't require any knowledge of the passage or any special preparation, it can get people talking and can help them to warm up to each other.

Second, an approach question can motivate people to study the passage at hand. At the beginning of the study, people in the group aren't necessarily ready to jump into the world of the Bible. Their minds may be on other things (their kids, a problem at work, an upcoming meeting) that have nothing to do with the study. An approach question can capture their interest and draw them into the discussion by raising important issues related to the study. The question becomes a bridge between their personal lives and the answers found in Scripture.

Third, a good approach question can reveal where people's thoughts or feelings need to be transformed by Scripture. That is why it is important to ask the approach question *before* reading the passage. The passage might inhibit the spontaneous, honest answers people might have given, because they feel compelled to give biblical answers. The approach question allows them to compare their personal thoughts and feelings with what they later discover in Scripture.

Question 2. Notice that we are to rejoice in the *Lord,* not necessarily in the circumstances that surround us. Christians in Paul's day faced persecutions and difficulties of various sorts. Paul himself was writing as a prisoner in Rome. But whatever our circumstances, we always have reason to rejoice in our relationship with God through Jesus Christ. God's grace is always sufficient for every situation we face.

Question 3. Paul uses several key words in verse 6: "'Prayer' denotes the petitioner's attitude of mind as worshipful. 'Petition' denotes prayers as expressions of need. 'Thanksgiving' should accompany all Christian praying, as the supplicant acknowledges that whatever God sends is for his good. It may also include remembrance of previous blessings. 'Requests' refers to the things asked for" (Homer A. Kent Jr., *Philippians,* The Expositor's Bible Commentary [Grand Rapids, Mich.: Zondervan, 1978], 152).

Question 4. Anxiety can distort our perspective, causing us to focus exclusively on our problems and our fears. Paul realizes that during such times we need to move our focus away from our fears and onto God. Likewise, we need to redirect our thinking away from our problems to all of the good things that God has done and is doing in our lives—even in the midst of our struggles. This isn't escapism; it is a matter of healthy balance and perspective.

Question 5. An anxious person tries over and over again to figure out a solution to what is making him anxious. When no solution is found, the mental process repeats and rerepeats in a futile cycle of anxiety. God's peace is not dependent on our figuring out a solution to what bothers us, nor is it dependent on our understanding how God will solve our problem. In fact, his help is often beyond our comprehension.

Question 6. Thankfulness (v. 6) and positive thoughts (v. 8) are two defenses against anxiety. Thankfulness reminds us of all the good things in our lives and helps put our problems in perspective. Positive thoughts can free our minds from being obsessively focused on whatever makes us anxious. (See also note to question 4.)

Questions 8–9. Paul knows that it is not enough for us to think about positive thoughts in the abstract. We must also follow the concrete example of godly Christians we know and admire.

"The four verbs in this verse form two pairs. The first pair, 'learned' and 'received,' describes the Philippians' instruction by Paul, from whom they had been taught Christian doctrine and Christian living. The next pair, 'heard' and 'saw,' depicts their personal observation of the apostle—both his speech and his conduct. As Ralph Martin aptly remarks, in the early days of the church before the NT writings were written or widely circulated, the standards of Christian belief and behavior were largely taught by being embodied in the words and example of the apostles (*The Epistle of Paul to the Philippians* [Grand Rapids: Eerdmans, 1959], 173.) Those who follow this apostolic guidance have the additional promise that God, who provides true peace (v. 9; cf. v. 7), will be with them" (Kent, *Philippians,* 152–53).

Study 2

WHY WE SHOULDN'T WORRY

Matthew 6:25–34

Purpose: To understand why Jesus tells us not to worry.

Question 2. D. A. Carson writes, "The point here is not to worry about the physical necessities, let alone the luxuries implied in the preceding verses, because such fretting suggests that our entire existence focuses on and is limited to such things. The argument is *a fortiori* ('how much more'). . . . If God has given us life and a body, both admittedly more important than food and clothing, will he not also give us the latter? Therefore fretting about such things betrays the loss of faith and the perversion of more valuable commitments" (cf. Luke 10:41–42; Heb. 13:5–6) (D. A. Carson, *Matthew,* The Expositor's Bible Commentary [Grand Rapids, Mich.: Zondervan, 1984], 179).

Question 3. Don't pass over this question too quickly. Imagine, for example, that you are very poor and have only simple, basic food to eat and old, worn-out clothes to wear. What other, more important things in life could still bring you great satisfaction and joy?

Question 4. Jesus uses two arguments from the lesser to the greater: If God feeds the birds of the air and clothes the lilies of the field—which are of far less value to God than we are—how much more will he feed and clothe us? His logic presupposes a view of the world in which God is intimately involved in every aspect of life—including the care and feeding of birds.

Question 5. This is a difficult question, but it is worth wrestling with. Some possible options are: (1) We can expect Christ's promises to be completely fulfilled now if we seek God's kingdom and righteousness.

This option, however, has insurmountable difficulties. It forces us to conclude that those who lack food and clothing are simply not seeking the Lord, a conclusion that conflicts with both Scripture and experience. (2) We can only expect Christ's promises to be fulfilled in the future, when the kingdom of God is fully established on earth. Yet this answer does not do justice to the intent of the passage, for Jesus is speaking to people who had immediate needs for food and clothing. (3) We can expect Christ's promises to be fulfilled in part now because God does care about and provide for our basic needs. But we will see the complete fulfillment of the promises only when he returns and his kingdom is fully established. Only then, for example, will our clothing surpass Solomon's.

Frederick Dale Bruner writes, "Only when we have been liberated from anxiety about our own food and clothes—a liberation devoutly to be desired in Western Christendom—will we give necessary attention to the food and clothing of the Poor World around us. Thus Jesus' text is not antisocial; it is antiselfish. It does not tell us to be unanxious about other's food, but to be unanxious about our own. It does not preach indifference to society; it preaches a rejection of Christians' unbelieving anxiety about themselves and their circumscribed obsessions. Anxious care is the denial of God; it is acting as if we are alone in the world and that either there is no God or that he does not care" (*The Christbook* [Waco, Tex.: Word Books, 1987], 266).

Question 8. Jesus is saying more than simply "the pagans run after these things" (v. 32). Rather, such pursuits can become a form of paganism when we elevate material concerns (food and clothing) above spiritual concerns (seeking Christ's kingdom and righteousness).

Question 9. "In view of vv. 31–32, this verse makes it clear that Jesus' disciples are not simply to *refrain* from the *pursuit* of temporal things as their primary goal in order to differentiate themselves from pagans. Instead, they are to *replace* such pursuits with goals of far greater significance.

"To seek first the kingdom ('of God' in some MSS) is to desire above all to enter into, submit to, and participate in spreading the news of the saving reign of God, the messianic kingdom already inaugurated by Jesus, and to live so as to store up treasures in heaven in the prospect of the kingdom's consummation. It is to pursue the things already prayed for in the first three petitions of the Lord's Prayer (6:9–10)" (D. A. Carson, *Matthew*, 181–82).

Commenting on this verse, John Stott writes, "In the end, just as there are only two kinds of piety, the self-centered and the God-centered, so there are only two kinds of ambition: one can be ambitious either for oneself or for God. There is no third alternative" (*The Message of the Sermon on the Mount* [Downers Grove, Ill.: InterVarsity, 1978], 172).

Study 3

FINDING PEACE IN GOD'S PRESENCE

Psalm 46

Purpose: To discover how the peace of God can be like a quiet refuge in the midst of a storm.

Question 2. Derek Kidner writes, "Luther's battle-hymn, *Ein'feste Burg,* took its starting-point from this psalm, catching its indomitable spirit but striking out in new directions. The psalm for its part proclaims the ascendancy of God in one sphere after another: His power over nature (1–3), over the attackers of His city (4–7) and over the whole warring world (8–11). Its robust, defiant tone suggests that it was composed at a time of crisis, which makes the confession of faith doubly impressive" (*Psalms 1–72,* Tyndale Old Testament Commentaries [Downers Grove, Ill.: InterVarsity, 1973], 174).

Question 3. Throughout this study, encourage the group to use their imaginations—to see God as a mighty fortress, to feel the vibrations as the earth shakes, to hear the roar as the waves break and the mountains crash into the sea. The author uses powerful imagery that can only work with our active participation.

Question 5. The "city of God" (v. 4) refers primarily to Jerusalem, the earthly dwelling place of God at the time this psalm was written. Although Jerusalem had no river like the cities of Thebes, Damascus, Babylon, or Nineveh, God himself was their river, providing them with constant spiritual refreshment even in the midst of a crisis. Later biblical authors pick up this theme and describe the river flowing through the heavenly Jerusalem (see Rev. 22:1–2). In a personal sense, however, the promises of the psalm are not tied to an earthly or heavenly location but assure us of God's presence with his people at all times and places. "Break of day" (v. 5) describes the time when armies normally attacked a city.

Question 6. "OT battle stories have as one of their staples fortresses—thick-walled cities, often on high mountains, meant to be impenetrable and intimidating to enemies. Yet of the approximately thirty-five references to fortresses in English Bibles, most are metaphoric pictures of God and his acts of salvation. . . . When David and other OT writers call God their fortress, they primarily picture God as the unshakable strength of their souls, the source of hope and salvation that no enemy—physical or spiritual—can ever threaten" (*Dictionary of Biblical Imagery*, Eds. Leland Ryken, James C. Wilhoit, Tremper Longman III [Downers Grove, Ill.: InterVarsity, 1998], 304–5).

Question 9. The command to "be still" (or "Enough!") is addressed primarily to the restless and turbulent world of wars and earthquakes. It resembles Christ's command to the storm (see Mark 4:35–41). Yet it includes the anxious as well, for we too need to learn that the Lord is God (v. 10) and that he will be exalted among us as he brings peace to our chaotic world.

Question 10. Don't force people in the group to reveal their personal battles—unless they do so voluntarily. For those in groups that have met for a long time, such personal sharing may be appropriate. For those who do not know each other well, it might be best to think about the battles silently and then share how this psalm can renew our trust in God.

Study 4

FEELING SAFE IN GOD'S CARE

Psalm 91

Purpose: To consider how we can feel safe in God's care in a world where bad things happen even to the faithful.

Question 1. Be sensitive to the fact that some members of your group may not have felt safe as children, especially if they came from abusive homes. If this question might create problems for your group, then modify it and ask, "What places or people help you to feel safe and secure?"

Question 2. The word *shelter* (v. 1) may be a reference to the temple. However, it is God's shelter, a place of refuge. The Lord is also described as a refuge (v. 2), a fortress (v. 2), a mother bird (v. 4), a shield (v. 4), and a dwelling (v. 9).

In addition to these images, the psalmist uses four divine names. Derek Kidner writes, "It is an eloquent opening, enriched not only by the four metaphors for security but by the four divine names. *Most High* is a title which cuts every threat down to size; *Almighty* (Shaddai) is the name which sustained the homeless patriarchs (Ex. 6:3). By the further appellation, *The Lord* (Yahweh), Moses was assured that 'I am' and 'I am with you' (Ex. 3:14, 12 NEB); while even the general term 'God' is made intimate by the possessive, as *my God*" (*Psalms 73–150,* Tyndale Old Testament Commentaries [Downers Grove, Ill.: InterVarsity, 1975], 332).

Notice that the psalmist begins with a personal affirmation of faith (vv. 1–2): "*I* will say of the LORD, 'He is *my* refuge and *my* fortress.'" Then he addresses the reader (vv. 3–13): "Surely he will save *you* from the fowler's snare" (italics mine). Finally, the Lord himself speaks both to the psalmist and to us (vv. 14–16): "'Because he loves me,' says the LORD, 'I will rescue him; I will protect him.'"

Question 3. In other words, what feelings of safety do you associate with God's being a refuge, a shield, a mother bird, and so on? Each image has its own connotations.

Questions 5–6. This is a difficult question, one not fully answered by the psalm itself. Clearly, the psalmist is not promising freedom from all adversity, for he mentions terrors, arrows, pestilence, plague, battles, disasters, snakes, and so on. Yet if this psalm were our only guide, it would seem to promise that none of these things will hurt us. However, this psalm is not our only guide. Other passages of Scripture must also be considered, including those that describe the sufferings of Christ. When taken together, the most that can be said is that nothing harmful will happen to us unless the Lord allows it.

Question 7. The words *dwelling* and *refuge* indicate an intimate and ongoing relationship with the Lord. We dwell in his presence and constantly seek his protection.

Notice that in verses 2 and 9 the psalmist makes a personal statement of faith: "He is my refuge and my fortress" (v. 2); "the LORD, who is my refuge" (v. 9). The psalmist knows God's protection from personal experience and urges us to seek the same care and protection.

Question 9. As a follow-up question, you might ask, "What specific promises does the Lord make to you in verses 14–16?"

Study 5

LIVING AT PEACE WITH OTHERS

Romans 12:17–21

Purpose: To learn to live at peace with others by overcoming evil with good.

Question 4. The first qualification indicates that there may be times when peace is not possible, in spite of our best efforts and intentions. The second qualification points out that peace requires both parties and, therefore, does not depend entirely on us.

Questions 5–6. "'Leave room for God's wrath' (v. 19). Trust him to take care of the situation. . . . Here Paul quotes Deuteronomy 32:35, whose context indicates that the Lord will intervene to vindicate his people when their enemies abuse them and gloat over them. . . . There is no suggestion that the wrath of God will be visited upon the wrongdoer immediately. On the contrary, that wrath is the last resort, for in the immediate future lies the possibility that the one who has perpetrated the wrong will have a change of heart and will be convicted of his sin and won over by the refusal of the Christian to retaliate (v. 20)" (Everett F. Harrison, *Romans,* The Expositor's Bible Commentary [Grand Rapids, Mich.: Zondervan, 1976], 135).

Question 7. Douglas Moo writes that "providing for an enemy's hunger and thirst is similar to the actions Jesus requires of us in response to an enemy: turning the other cheek, giving our shirts to those who ask for our coats, and giving to those who beg from us (Luke 6:29–30)" (*Romans,* NIV Application Commentary series, ed. Terry Muck [Grand Rapids: Zondervan, 2000], 413).

Question 8. "*Heap burning coals on his head.* Horrible punishment reserved for the wicked (see Ps. 140:10). Here, however, it is kindness that will hurt the enemy (cf. the broken bone of v. 15) but perhaps win him over. Alternatively, the expression may reflect an Egyptian expiation ritual, in which a guilty person, as a sign of his repentance, carried a basin of glowing coals on his head. The meaning here, then, would be that in returning good for evil and so being kind to your enemy, you may cause him to repent or change" (*The NIV Study Bible* [Grand Rapids, Mich.: Zondervan, 1985], note to Proverbs 25:22).

Study 6

CHRIST, OUR PEACE

Ephesians 2:11–22

Purpose: To realize that Christ has demolished the barriers that divide us.

Introduction. Huck's response to Aunt Sally reveals the terrible racial prejudice of that period. Huck not only refers to the dead man as a "nigger," an obviously degrading label, but also views him as less than human (*no one* was killed—just a nigger).

Question 3. "The apostle urges the Ephesians to recollect what they once were in their heathen state. Four successive phrases depict their debits as compared with those of the Jews (cf. Rom. 9:4, 5). In the first place, they were without or apart (NIV, 'separate') from Christ. They had no expectation of a Messiah to light up their darkness. They knew nothing at all about him. They had no rights of citizenship (*politea*) in his kingdom. They were cut off from any such privilege by reason of their birth. . . . They lived in a world devoid of hope (1 Thess. 4:13). They were, moreover, 'without God' (*atheoi*). This does not imply that they were forsaken by God, but that, since they were ignorant of him (Gal. 4:8), they did not believe in him" (A. Skevington Wood, *Ephesians,* The Expositor's Bible Commentary [Grand Rapids, Mich.: Zondervan, 1978], 38–39).

Question 5. Paul describes the separation between Jews and Gentiles as a "barrier" and as a "dividing wall of hostility" (v. 14). "Josephus used each of these terms separately with reference to the balustrade in the Jerusalem temple separating the court of the Gentiles from the temple proper. On it was an inscription that read: 'No foreigner may enter within the barricade which surrounds the sanctuary and enclosure. Anyone who is caught doing so will have himself to blame for his ensuing death.'

"When Jerusalem fell in A.D. 70, this partition was demolished along with the temple itself. But Paul saw it as already destroyed by Christ at the cross" (A. Skevington Wood, *Ephesians,* 40).

Question 7. This question overlaps somewhat with question 5. However, it is good for the group to personalize Paul's statements, taking the references beyond Jews and Gentiles and applying them to those people from whom they feel alienated.

Questions 9–10. Very few churches have been able to successfully unite people from diverse ethnic, racial, and social backgrounds. One such church, Circle Church in Chicago, tried very hard to achieve a true interracial community, but their experiment ultimately failed. You might ask the group why such unity is so difficult, especially since Christ has made us one in him. Is it practical to hope for and work toward unity in diversity, or are our churches destined to remain homogeneous until Christ returns?

We want to hear from you. Please send your comments about this book to us in care of zreview@zondervan.com. Thank you.

ZONDERVAN.com/
AUTHORTRACKER
follow your favorite authors

Printed in the USA
CPSIA information can be obtained
at www.ICGtesting.com
LVHW020709050824
787165LV00009B/71

9 780310 238690